Stories For Change

Book 1

Telene Clarke

These stories are adaptations of traditional tales. The additional interpretations and comments are the work of the author and are therefore subject to copyright. They are not to be used without the permission of the author.

Copyright © 2014 Telene Clarke

All rights reserved.

ISBN:10: 1495305503
ISBN-13: 978-1495305504

ACKNOWLEDGMENTS

Thank you to those who
have allowed me the privilege of sharing a part of their
journey in life and in doing so, have given me firsthand
feedback
on the power of these tales.
Thanks to the health professionals, teachers and parents
who have helped me to trial these stories and who provided
invaluable advice as to their uses and effectiveness.
Sincere thanks also to those who have helped me to edit
and create this series of books.
Special thanks to:
Dr Caroline Wheeler for her help and advice.
Mary Gudzenovs for her technical assistance and endless
patience.
Carmen Southam, my favourite psycho…logist.
And Rae Clarke, Clare Andrews
and Michelle deVeau.
I couldn't have done it without you!

CONTENTS

	Introduction	P. 1
1.	The Hungry Leopard	P. 7
2.	Baking a Fish	P. 13
3.	Be Happy	P. 19
4.	Born to Fly	P. 25
5.	Destiny	P. 33
6.	Hairs	P. 39
7.	More Is Not Enough	P. 45
8.	Starfish	P. 51
9.	The Gift	P. 57
10.	The King And the Boulder	P. 63

11	Donkey	P. 69
12	Losing Everything	P. 75
13	Two Wolves	P. 81
14	What Would You Know?	P. 87
15	Duck And Chicken	P. 91
16	Fisherman	P. 99
17	Good Luck, Bad Luck	P. 107
18	The Six Blind Men and the Elephant	P. 113
19	What will It be Like?	P. 119
20	The Black Door	P. 125
	Quick Guide Index	P. 131

Introduction

Why use stories?

Very few of us enjoy being told what to do, but we do enjoy a good story!

The *good advice* we get often goes in one ear and out of the other, even when we recognise the value of it.

However, if a message comes wrapped up in a story that's humorous, inspirational, thought-provoking or simply entertaining, then we're much more likely to take the message on board and to apply it to our own everyday life.

It can be frustrating trying to get through to those who just don't seem willing to hear. We can lecture, we can educate, we can repeat it over and over, but sometimes it seems that the very people we want to help are incapable of taking in what they need to know.

Warn a teenager of life's perils and they'll shrug their shoulders and yawn. Tell them an entertaining story about someone else (not at all like them) who was faced with a situation (a little like theirs) and the message is a lot more likely to get through.

Stories provide a *one-step-removed* way to get a message across; a message designed to inspire, to encourage, to reassure or to connect someone to the resources or strategies they need to move ahead.

Often it can be difficult to pass on an experience or an understanding simply with words. By describing an experience that we can all relate to or empathise with, we can find a common thread that unites us and elicits an emotional response within us.

When we *feel,* we remember.

That emotional response helps to make stories *stick.* Often we'll remember a great story or a joke even if we have no idea who told it to us. Most of us can recall stories that were told or read to us as children, no matter how old we are.

Stories remain in our minds to be accessed when needed and are often handed along to help others.

What's different about this collection?

Traditional parables and moral stories are often delivered without explanation, with the belief that we will simply 'get them' at the unconscious level. Sometimes we do… and quite often we don't.

We walk out of the therapist's office or away from the motivational talk wondering what on earth a fox who eats grapes or a goose who can sing has to do with our problem with our boss at work. Sometimes we are left feeling quite stupid when we don't 'get it'.

INTRODUCTION

The fact is, most people are *literal* or *concrete thinkers* and many of us struggle to find meaning when stories seem a bit obscure or not relevant to our own lives. Sometimes we need a bit of help to join the dots.

When metaphors are combined with a brief discussion (as considered at the end of each tale in this book), the message can be much more powerful and the shifts in thinking much quicker and more profound. We can bring the story's message clearly into consciousness and begin becoming more aware of how it applies to our everyday life; almost immediately.

It fast-tracks our progress.

Stories can also be interpreted in many different ways. The same story can actually have completely contradictory messages depending on who we are, our life experiences, what challenges we are currently facing in life or how we choose to see that story in that moment.

By offering some possible themes and interpretations along with discussion points at the end of each tale, these stories can be used in specific contexts to address individual issues and to help direct people towards particular understandings and awareness.

Why these particular stories?

These simple stories are some that I have used and shared over 30 years of working with others. They are ideal for therapists, parents, teachers, public speakers or simply anyone who engages with people.

These stories are also for you. They will resonate and stay with you long after you have read them.

How to use these stories

The stories in these collections are designed to be told and are easy to memorise. They can be adapted, changed, made shorter or made more complex depending on who you are sharing them with.

There is no need to memorise them word for word; it is simply a matter of remembering the simple structure of the story, then relaying it in a way that feels natural to you.

Alternatively, they can be read aloud.

There are **discussion points** at the end of each tale based around possible themes and interpretations and also some suggestions about contexts or situations in which each story may be useful. This can help you to **select specific stories** for those facing particular issues or challenges.

This collection of stories has been collated with the assistance of a number of therapists, psychologists, doctors and parents who have provided invaluable feedback about each story's effectiveness and contexts in which it has proven useful. All have received positive feedback about patient and client responses and

INTRODUCTION

transformations.

I hope you get as much enjoyment and positive change from these tales as we have.

Happy reading!

Telene Clarke

TELENE CLARKE

1. The Hungry Leopard

Sometime, not too long ago, a lady went on a safari holiday to Africa.

The lady was very close to her little dog so she decided to take her along too.

One afternoon the pocket-sized dog wandered a little too far from the tents and found herself lost in the bush. She was looking around, trying to decide what to do next when she heard a rustling noise from behind. Glancing around, the tiny canine spotted a very hungry-looking leopard creeping stealthily towards her. Realising she was in big trouble, the little dog had to think fast. She noticed a pile of fresh-looking bones scattered on the ground nearby and quick as a flash she settled down to chew on them with her back to the big cat. Just as the leopard was about to spring the little dog smacked her lips loudly and exclaimed "Boy, that was one delicious leopard! I wonder if there are any more around here?"

The leopard caught himself in mid-stride and tiptoed off into the trees. "Phew," he said to himself, with a huge sigh of relief, when he was far enough away to feel safe again. "That was close! That evil little dog almost had me."

A monkey, who had been watching the whole thing from a nearby tree, thought he would turn the situation to his own advantage by telling the stupid leopard how he'd been duped by the pint-sized mutt.

The little dog noticed the monkey sneaking off after the leopard and guessed straight away that he was up to no good.

When the leopard heard the monkey's story he was furious about being made to look so foolish. Snarling fiercely, he vowed to get revenge. He invited the monkey to ride on his back so he could witness the payback. He was going to show that dog that nobody messes with a leopard!

The little dog, still trying to figure out which direction to head in, heard them coming and feared the worst. Again she had to think fast. Once more she turned her back and pretended not to notice the pair as they approached, waiting until they were just within earshot before saying loudly "Now, where's that monkey got to? I sent him off ages ago to find me another leopard."

(Source: Unknown)

Possible themes in this story:

Fake it 'til you make it. Life is a game of bluff. Be **bold**.

We can be terrified on the inside but it's what presents itself on the outside that counts in so many situations. It is the **mask** or **persona** that we present to the outside world that ensures our results. Often our **courage** and **confidence** starts with *pretending* to be courageous and confident.

Act with **courage** and **confidence** in the face of **fear** and we really get to see what we're capable of.

Courage - Not giving in to fear. All of us are afraid at times. We can allow fear to paralyse us or we can use it to motivate ourselves into taking **positive action**.

Size is not important – small does not mean weak.

Attitude is everything. Even when faced with enormous adversity, our attitude is the telling point. We can be beaten and resign ourselves to failure or we can believe we can keep going. If the dog had believed she was going to be eaten, she wouldn't have lasted three seconds.

Self-belief - Keep on believing in yourself no matter what.

Anger vs 'being smart'. Smart thinking is what keeps us safe. In challenging situations **intelligence** is what helps rather than reacting emotionally.

Keeping a cool head.

Intelligence beats brawn. Smart beats power. (Power doesn't necessarily make you smart!)

We can cry, feel sorry for ourselves, get angry, be fearful or we can simply use what we already know and be **smart**.

Likewise, we can **react emotionally** or we can **do** something.

The something we do always begins with a thought and a **choice**.

We can see a **problem** or we can see a **solution**. It really depends on what we're looking for.

Creative thinking - **Lateral solutions**. Making use of what is around you to solve a problem. Having the ability to think outside of the square. The more **flexible** and innovative our thinking, the more options we give ourselves. The more **rigid** and **habitual** our **thinking** becomes, the more we limit our ability to **cope with change** or to find solutions to life's challenges.

Problem-solving and **decision-making**. Sometimes there is no time to **procrastinate.** We need to be able to solve-problems and make decisions quickly. The more we practice, the better we get.

Hope - There is always hope, even when the situation may appear hopeless! Retaining hope allows us to keep our **options** open, often allowing us to avert seemingly certain disaster.

Never give up!

This story may be useful for:

- When feeling like there's no way out of a situation- when a situation appears **hopeless.**
- When feeling **defeated** or beaten.
- In a situation where you feel another has the **upper hand**.
- Those who feel **powerless**, **intimidated** and outweighed by a **challenge**.
- People who don't believe they can **cope**.
- Feeling someone is more **powerful** than you.
- Encouraging **creative thinking.**
- Encouraging **problem solving skills** and **flexibility** in thinking.
- Kids who are **small in size,** especially boys who are of small stature. People who *feel* small, **weak** or **powerless**.
- When being **bullied.**

- ➢ To keep **safe** in **unsafe situations** - eg **child protection** . Quite often the only way out of a situation is to use a combination of intuition and being smart. Set up the idea of being able to think on your feet when faced with danger and then to act fast.

- ➢ **Procrastinators** - (they would be eaten in the first two minutes!)

- ➢ Remember, sometimes all you have to **believe** is the **possibility** of an option for one to open up.

- ➢ Just thinking of the dog gives you **courage** and changes your thinking.

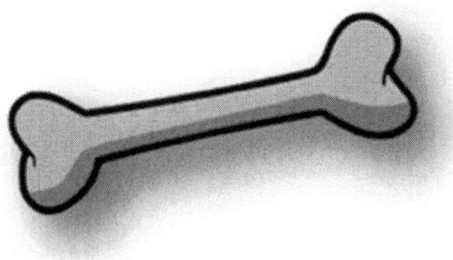

2. Baking A Fish

One day a little girl was watching her mother prepare fish for the evening meal. As usual her mother cut off the head and then the tail of the fish before she placed it into the big baking pan.

"Why do you always cut the head and the tail off the fish?" asked the little girl curiously.

Her mother thought for a while then said "Well, I'm not really sure. I've always done it that way because I guess that's how my mother showed me. Why don't we ask her when she comes for dinner tonight?"

That evening the little girl climbed onto her grandmother's knee. "Grandma, how come you always cut the head and the tail off the fish before you bake it?"

"Well," said the Grandmother, her brow furrowing as she thought. "I'm not sure. I guess that's just how my mother taught me."

The little girl was now even more determined to know why and so the next day she asked her mother if they could visit her Great-Grandmother to see if she knew the answer.

Great Grandmother was quite old by now and lived in a retirement home.

As soon as they got there the little girl ran straight up to the old woman.

"Great Grandma! Great Grandma! Please tell me, why did you always cut the head and the tail off the fish before you baked it?"

Great Grandmother thought for a moment and then replied: "Why? It was because my baking pan was way too small to fit a whole fish into."

"Oh," said the girl, "I see…"

(Source: Unknown)

Possible themes in this story:

Habits - Most of the things we do, we do without even thinking. We have very little conscious **awareness** around the everyday actions we perform and around our **thinking** patterns, our **attitudes** and **behaviours**. This can lead to some of those habits being not very logical, helpful or useful to us anymore, but we keep on doing things the same old way for the simple reason that we've always done it that way!

Sometimes we get so caught up in **routine** that we don't even notice what we're doing.

Family beliefs - How many things are passed onto us by our families without us ever questioning them?

Sometimes they may be simple things like the way we bake a fish but there may be deeper level beliefs around important things like:

- **relationships** (Eg: *The man always makes the important decisions.*)
- **money** (Eg: *Money is hard to come by.*)
- **self-worth** *(Eg: No-one in this family is smart enough to go to university.)* Sometimes we may not even recognise these beliefs because they are so familiar and 'normal' that we never think to question them.

Tradition - Just because some things have always been done in a certain way, it doesn't necessarily follow that they should continue to be done that way. What we do may no longer be relevant, logical or useful. Many traditions (including family ones) began so long ago that their initial purpose and meaning has been lost. **Awareness** allows us **choice** about determining whether things are still **useful** or r**elevant** to us.

Learning - When we keep our minds open to learning we realise that it is a lifetime process. There are always new things to learn and better ways to go about things. By being open and willing to take on **new ideas**, to experiment and be creative we are constantly opening up new **neural pathways** and expanding our **possibilities** and opportunities.

Mindfulness - If we do things 'mindfully' we have the ability to question their relevance and usefulness. Mindfulness allows us **choice**.

Assumptions - Quite often the assumptions we make are completely wrong.

Curiosity - With age many of us lose the curiosity of childhood. Retaining a sense of curiosity allows us to experience life more fully and to actually **be present** in it.

Curiosity reminds us to ask **questions** and keep asking until we get the information we need.

It's okay to question. Good questions are much more important than good answers.

It's all about **context**. Just because something works in one context that does not mean it will work in another context. Often we tend to **generalise** and fall into a **'one-size-fits-all' type of thinking**. This type of thinking can **limit** us. By being **flexible** and open to new ways of doing things it becomes quicker and **easier** to find better ways of doing things.

This story may be useful for:

- When needing more **flexibility** and an ability to **think critically**, to question and to be mindful about the things we do.

- **Habits** - When someone is repeating habits, doing the same things over and over or repeating the same **mistakes** again and again.

- People who get into **destructive patterns** in life. Those who keep repeating behaviours that are not useful or are even harmful to them. They may have an awareness of this but have no idea *why* they keep doing the same old destructive things.

- When someone is **not acting mindfully**; not bringing conscious awareness into their lives.

- When a person is not having **awareness** around their own behaviours, beliefs and attitudes.

- Someone who is **stuck** in a rut.

- When someone is being **resistant to change**.

- For those caught up in destructive or damaging family behaviours and belief systems.

3. Be Happy

Once there was a little boy who started at the local kindergarten. He was a serious young fellow who never seemed to smile very much. The adults around him asked what he needed to be happy. "I won't be happy until I get to school where I can do more things," replied the little boy.

Soon he began Primary School, where the other kids were having lots of fun, but still the boy rarely seemed to smile or laugh. "When will you be happy?' asked his teachers. "I will not be happy until I finish here and get into High School where I can do some *real* learning," replied the boy.

Soon enough the boy began High School. The other kids were enjoying being teenagers but the boy was still not happy. "I won't be happy until I can get out of here and do my own thing at University," he told himself.

University was a great social experience for most of the students. It was a time of experimentation and spreading of wings, but not for the boy. "I will not be happy until I have my degree," he told anyone who would listen.

After four years, with his degree in his hand, the boy

realised he couldn't possibly be happy until he had a good job. Of course as soon as he found a job, he realised that he was starting right at the bottom of the pile and that he couldn't possibly be happy until he'd worked his way up the company ladder.

The years passed and the boy, who was by now of course a man, worked his way up through the company telling himself at each step: "I'll be happy when I get married… when I can afford a good house… when I have children… when the children finish school… when I manage this company…when I….."

It took many years, but sure enough, eventually he worked his way to the top of the company. His children had left home. "Aaahh," he said, "Almost there."

"All I have to do now is to wait until it's time to retire then I can put my feet up, relax and I can finally be happy."

Eventually the day came when it was time for the man to retire…….

The next day he died.

(Source: Adaptation of Old Sufi Story)

BE HAPPY

Possible themes in this story:

The only time to be **happy** is **now**.

Too many of us **postpone our happiness**.

Waiting - We put our lives on hold waiting for something better to come along, waiting for something to change, waiting for someone to rescue us, a golden opportunity to arise. We live powerless lives waiting for external factors to *make* us happy. As if it is something that happens *to* us.

Many of us link happiness to the **attainment of things**; material things, wealth, status, our careers. Often these things give us short-term satisfaction, but in the next moment our attention turns to what we can have or achieve next. Consequently the pursuit of *things* rarely makes us happy.

Likewise many of us link our own happiness to **others**, the people around us. We depend on them for our own happiness, to *make* us happy.

We then **blame** and complain when things don't go as planned; when they don't make us as happy as they should.

A reminder that happiness is generated from **inside** and the only one who has any control over that is us. It is through the way we think, our attitudes and how we choose to do things that we create our own happiness.

The only way we can be truly happy is to take **responsibility for our own happiness**.

We can pursue happiness or we can make a simple **choice** to begin being happy right now.

Action - We need to take action to create our own happiness. We can choose to be active participants in the process instead of seeing ourselves as passive recipients.

We need to acknowledge the real things that create happiness and that requires us to **re-evaluate** occasionally. Things like **time for ourselves** and sharing time with family and friends doing things that relax and energise us. Otherwise life simply passes us by and so does happiness.

This story may be useful for:

- **Unhappy** people. Those who refuse to be happy no matter what.

- **Consumers** - Those addicted to acquiring 'stuff'. Compulsive shoppers. Those who want the latest, the best, or what the neighbours next door have.

- **Workaholics** - People who lose sight of what they're actually working *for*.

- **Parents** who need to be reminded to spend more **time with their children.**

- **Busy** people. Those who are so busy attending to the **urgent** things that they forget all about the **important** things.

- Those who **make excuses**. Those who always have a reason why they can't possibly….

- **Procrastinators** - Those who talk but do not **do**.

- Those who are **waiting**, living their **life on hold**; who convince themselves that happiness is just around the next corner.

- **Men** in particular often excuse their focus on **work and career** as being *for* their family, often at the expense of spending precious time *with* their family.

- Those who **blame** and complain rather than **taking responsibility** for their own lives.

4. Born To Fly

One day a boy decided to go exploring. He was walking along enjoying the sunshine when he came to a large, shady tree. He sat down in the soft grass beneath the tree and rested his back against the rough bark of the trunk. As he sat listening to the sounds of the birds and the bees and the other insects he noticed a small, finely crafted cocoon hanging suspended from a twig.

Leaning in closer, the boy saw a tiny opening in the cocoon and realised that a butterfly was attempting to leave its encasement and come into the world.

He sat mesmerised, watching the feeble creature as it struggled to force its body through the tiny hole. It would struggle then stop, struggle then stop, as if exhausted from the effort. Again and again the tiny creature would expend energy and effort and then stop as if defeated, looking as if it was unable to continue.

As he watched this struggle the boy became more and more concerned.

Finally, after witnessing the battle over a period of time, he could restrain himself no longer.

He decided that he would assist the butterfly's entrance into the world by helping her out of her cocoon.

Carefully, using the small knife he kept in his pocket, he gently cut away at the cocoon until the casing fell away and the soggy butterfly was exposed to the world.

He watched expectantly, waiting in anticipation for the butterfly to unfurl herself and stretch out her wings and fly, but instead she became gradually more and more still until, shortly after, her body became limp and lifeless.

Now the boy felt very upset about this. He ran and ran all of the way home. Finding his Grandmother he tearfully related the story to her. "What had gone wrong?", he asked her.

The boy's Grandmother took him on her knee and explained that the butterfly's struggle to force itself through the tiny opening of its cocoon, is nature's way of forcing the fluid from the butterfly's body into its wings in order for it to be ready to take flight.

Sometimes, explained the Grandmother, we need to experience some hardships in order to spread our wings and fly.

(Source: Unknown)

Possible themes in this story:

At times, we may find we **are** the butterfly, or we may find ourselves as the one who wants to **help** the butterfly....

As the butterfly:

Having **struggles** and **challenges** are a normal part of life. We are all going to face situations that are difficult and uncomfortable. Sometimes it will require a lot of **effort** and hard work to get through those hard times, but there is usually a **reward** at the end if we look for it; just like the butterfly's reward for its struggle is the joy of flight.

In struggle we get to develop **resilience**, the ability to bounce back from tough situations. That often allows us to **cope** more easily with any future challenges we may have.

We get to build **courage** and to **feel good about ourselves**. The feeling of having successfully navigated our way through a tough situation by ourselves, can often be a real turning point for many people.

Like the butterfly, sometimes **hardships** and struggle are what we most need in life, although that may be very difficult to accept at the time. It may be only in hindsight that we can go back and view the struggle in order to **reframe** the situation and see it in a completely new way. We can only then recognise the positive outcomes or benefits that were gained from the experience.

There are **opportunities for learning** in everything that happens. Instead of reacting because things have not gone the way we had hoped or **expected,** it is useful to stop and ask ourselves what we have learned from this experience. Have you ever been through something that seemed terrible at the time, but down the track turned into the best thing that could have happened? Struggles and challenges can **appear bad** at the time, but later on we realise that they were the things that helped make us who we are; that taught us to access our **inner strengths**, that gave us **important lessons** that we'll always remember and that opened up new **opportunities** that we hadn't been aware of before.

Challenges are what allow us to access those parts of ourselves that allow us to be strong and thrive.

Often those **inner strengths** and **resources** remain hidden from us until called upon in times of adversity. It is only through having the courage and the **determination** to find our own way out of our cocoons that we can truly access our true **potential** and **transform** ourselves into all that we can be.

Just like the transformation from caterpillar to butterfly, we need to go through a **transformative process** in our journey to become **wiser**, **smarter**, **better** people. That process can often be tough, requiring **effort**, **commitment**, **dedication** and **discomfort**.

That is how we **learn** and **grow**.

Discomfort may not feel very pleasant, but it allows us to learn and to flourish. It is important to remember that **discomfort is temporary** and necessary for our growth. Being willing to experience discomfort is essential for personal growth.

Butterfly 'Helpers'

Some of us are born **helpers** or **rescuers**.

We feel good when we **fix things** for others; when we make things 'right' or 'better'.

Sometimes we can see the potential in others and we are attempting to help them to transform.

However, in helping, we can often unintentionally **hinder** the progress of those we care about. By constantly **rescuing** others we can **deprive** them of opportunities to learn skills and life lessons that they need for their own personal success and happiness.

Leaping in to **save** them might make us feel good for a while, but often keeps them trapped in patterns of behavior and situations that are not helpful for them. Helping can in fact **prolong a negative situation** for the person being 'helped'.

Allowing others their own journey and their own lessons can be difficult at times, but it may be the biggest gift we can give them.

Instead of jumping in early, sometimes we simply need to stop and assess the situation fully. Then we can make an informed decision about when and *if* we actually need to help. We can notice whether the decision to help is actually about them, or more about **making ourselves feel good**.

Parents - When the butterfly we are trying to rescue is our child or a family member, it can be extremely challenging to allow them to struggle or to make mistakes.

Sometimes, those times when it appears that others **need us** most, what they most need is to be **left alone.**

Sometimes, in our desire to be **kind** and to help others, we actually do them more **harm** than good.

And sometimes, helping others is more about making ourselves feel good, without us stopping to take time to understand the effect of our desire to be helpful on those we are helping.

Control - Some of us like to be in control of the things that happen to us and around us. This is not always possible. Some things are simply out of our hands. In these situations we need to practice **acceptance**.

Acceptance - Sometimes things do not go as we would like them to, and quite often there is a reason for that. We need to know what is 'our business' and what belongs to others.

Real learning comes from us experiencing things

firsthand. Quite often those things present in the form of a life challenge.

When we think about our major life lessons, for many of us, they have been the things that we have experienced directly, not simply things others have told us about. Trying to pass what we've learnt onto others rarely has the same impact as allowing them to experience it for themselves. It is only when the toddler reaches out and touches the stove that they really understand what the word 'hot' means.

This story may be useful for:.

- **Helpers** and **Rescuers**

- Fearful 'helicopter parents' who are **protecting** their **children** from life experiences.

- When facing **adversity** or life **challenges.**

- Those who try to **fix** everyone but themselves.

- Building **resilience.**

- **Normalising struggle** as a **temporary** part of life.

- **Reframing** situations that may appear 'bad'. (Finding the silver lining in the situation.)

- **Negative** thinkers.

- Those prone to **victim thinking.**

- When we need to practice **patience** and **allowance**, giving others the space to move forward at their own pace.

5. Destiny

It was a significant battle and the soldiers were nervous. The General made the decision to launch an attack against the enemy, even though it was quite obvious that his army was greatly outnumbered. He was confident they would win but his men were filled with doubt. Despite the General's confidence in them, the talk of the soldiers was full of fear and uncertainty.

On the way to the battle, they stopped at a religious shrine. After praying with the men, the General took out a coin and said:

"I shall now toss this coin. If it is heads, we shall win. If tails, we shall lose. Destiny will now reveal itself."

He threw the coin high into the air and all watched keenly as it landed. It was heads.

The soldiers were so overjoyed and filled with confidence that they were unstoppable. They forcefully attacked the enemy and were, of course, victorious.

After the battle, as the Officers gathered in celebration, a Lieutenant approached the General and remarked knowingly, "No one can change destiny."

"Quite right," the General replied.

He pulled the coin from his pocket and showed it to the Lieutenant.

As he looked at the coin that rested in the General's hand the Lieutenant's jaw dropped in surprise.

On both sides of the coin….. was a head.

(Source: Zen Parable)

Possible themes in this story:

Choice - Life is about choices. The choices we make determine our **outcomes**.

Allowing **destiny** or **fate** to govern our lives, surrendering to outside forces, disempowers us and leaves us at the mercy of factors outside of ourselves. It is only by taking **responsibility** for ourselves, for our thoughts, our attitudes and our choices, that we ensure our success in life.

Putting our faith in things outside of us **disempowers** us. It is as fickle and unpredictable as the toss of a coin.

Decision making - We can make decisions or we can allow them to be made for us.

The power of belief - What we believe and tell ourselves has a direct bearing on what happens for us. So often our thoughts and words become a self-fulfilling prophecy.

The *Placebo Effect* directly influences our **results** constantly. What we believe becomes our truth.

Belief is a very powerful thing!

What we **think** determines what we **do**. Our actions and our outcomes in life stem directly from our ways of thinking.

Courage - If we have enough **trust** in ourselves and

self-belief we can do anything. Having the courage to step through **fear** to success is often as simple as a modest change in our thinking about a situation.

Self-empowerment. Making the choice to take charge of our own lives.

Being **mindful** with what we fill our head with. Becoming aware of our thoughts, our beliefs and our attitudes and taking responsibility for them.

Negative thinking *vs* **Positive thinking** - If we think we can, we can. If we think we can't, we can't.

Confidence can only come from the inside. It is the starting point for success.

Attitude is everything. It takes us down or brings us up. It becomes the blueprint for our **success** or our **failure** and is decided by us.

This story may be useful for:

- Emphasising the **power of belief** and how to use this to our advantage.

- Someone who fails to take **action.**

- Those who see life as something that happens *to* them. Who believe that life is outside of their control.

- Times when feeling **defeated.**

- When a situation appears **hopeless.**

- When feeling **powerless.**

- When facing a **challenge** that feels **overwhelming** or scary.

- When needing to make a choice or **decision** that appears out of our **control.**

- As a reminder to choose our **thoughts** and words with care.

- Those who make **excuses.**

TELENE CLARKE

6. Hairs

Once upon a time there was a very old lady.

One morning she got up and looked into the mirror to find that she had only three hairs remaining on her head.

Being a positive sort of person she thought for a moment then declared: "Hmmm, I think I'll plait my hair today."

She plaited her hair and had a great day.

The very next morning, looking in the mirror and preparing for her day, the very old lady noticed that she now had only two hairs remaining on her head. "Hmmm, two hairs, I think I fancy a part down the middle today."

She carefully parted her two hairs and, as ever, she had a great day.

At sunrise the following day the old lady awoke to discover that she finally had only one remaining hair on her head. "Hmmm," she mused, " One hair, I know! A ponytail will be just fine!" and yet again she had the most wonderful day.

On the fourth morning, as usual, the very old woman looked into the mirror.

She saw that she was completely bald.

"Hmmm, finally bald huh?" she said to herself. "How perfectly wonderful! Now I won't have to waste all of that time doing my hair every day."

(Source: Unknown)

Possible themes in this story:

Optimism - Having a **positive outlook** on life determines your everyday experiences. Ultimately, how we live our days is how we live our lives.

Perspective - Going bald may be a personal tragedy for some of us, but if it is a result of chemotherapy for example, it pales into insignificance compared to the big picture of the illness. Sometimes we spend so much time focused on the little things that we lose sight of the big picture.

Bad things happen, even to nice people. That's life. It's our **attitude** towards them that makes them either bigger and worse or smaller and less significant.

Negative Thinking and **Choice** - We can suck on the lemons or we can make lemonade.

Gratitude for what you have as opposed to focusing on what you *don't* have.

Focus - We see what we look for. If we are looking for the negatives we will spot negatives. If we are looking for positives then that is what we will find.

Self-image - So much emphasis is put on self-image these days. Some of us become so obsessed with our perceived flaws, that we overlook the good things about ourselves.

Ageism - The wisdom of the elderly is something that is to be treasured.

Inspiration - Drawing personal inspiration from others. If the old woman can still be happy and see the positive in this situation then I can cope with the little things that come *my* way.

Letting go of worrying about the **opinions of others.** Too many of us spend an inordinate amount of our time being concerned about what we **believe** others think of us.

This story may be useful for:

- People who are continually worried about what **others may think** of them.

- **Pessimists/Negative thinkers** - Those who always see negative in a situation and are unable or unwilling to acknowledge anything positive.

- **Worriers** and those experiencing **anxiety.**

- **Focus** - Learning to focus on the positives. What you *do* have as opposed to what you do not.

- Those struggling with **perspective.** People who have lost sight of the important things in life and are all caught up in their own **problems**.

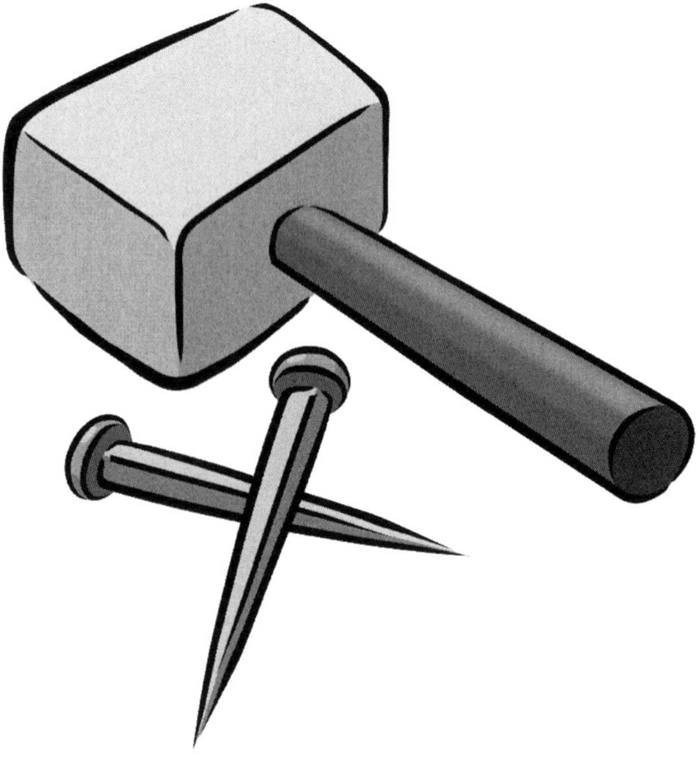

7. More Is Not Enough

There was once a stonecutter who was never content with his life. One day he passed a wealthy merchant's house. Through the open gateway, he saw many wonderful possessions and a host of important visitors. "How powerful that merchant must be!" thought the stonecutter. He became very envious and wished that he could be like the merchant.

To his surprise, he suddenly became the merchant, enjoying more luxuries and power than he had ever imagined, but envied and detested by those less wealthy than himself. Soon an important official passed by, carried high by his bearers, accompanied by attendants and escorted by soldiers beating drums. Everyone, no matter how wealthy, had to bow low before the procession. "How powerful that official is!" he thought. "I wish that I could be him!"

In a flash he became the important official, carried everywhere in his embroidered chair, feared and hated by the people all around. It was a hot summer's day, and the official soon began to feel very uncomfortable as the rays of the sun bore down on him. He looked up at the sun. It shone proudly in the sky, unaffected by his presence. "How powerful the sun is!" he thought. "I wish that I could be the sun!"

Suddenly he became the sun, shining fiercely down on everyone, scorching the fields, cursed by the farmers and laborers. He had never felt more powerful. But, just as he was enjoying being the mighty sun a huge black cloud moved between him and the earth, so that his light could no longer shine on everything below. "How powerful that storm cloud is!" he thought. "I wish that I could be a cloud!"

So he became the cloud, flooding the fields and villages with a torrent of water, shouted at by everyone. However, just as he was enjoying unleashing such a disturbance, he found that he was being pushed aside by some great force and realised that it was the wind. "How powerful it is!" he thought. "I wish that I could be the wind!"

He was immediately the wind, blowing tiles off the roofs of houses, uprooting trees, feared and hated by all below him. All that he encountered fell before him, but after a time he came up against something that would not move, no matter how forcefully he blew against it - a huge, towering rock. "How powerful that rock is!" he thought. "I wish that I could be a rock!"

Then he became the rock, more powerful than anything else on earth. But as he proudly stood there, he heard the sound of a hammer pounding a chisel into the hard surface, and felt himself being changed beyond his control. "What could be more powerful than I, the rock?" he thought.

He looked down and saw far below him the figure of a stonecutter.

(Source: Zen Parable)

Possible themes in this story:

Being **satisfied** with what we have.

Greed rarely makes us happy.

Happiness - Looking for it in what we perceive we *don't* have and then discovering that what we desired doesn't actually make us happy.

Searching for things that we already have.

Making the most of our **natural gifts** and **talents** instead of overlooking them.

We are all amazing, but often we don't see that. We are so busy **wanting what others have**, of thinking that others are better off than us. Eg: the talented musician who believes that she is 'stupid' because she finds mathematics difficult or the talented drawer who does everything but draw.

Quite often we are so focused on what we *don't* have that we forget to notice what we do have.

Familiarity often breeds contempt when it comes to ourselves. We get so used to what we do that we forget how well we do it and how skilled we are and difficult it may be for someone else.

Wanting more. The grass is always greener on the other side of the fence. The problem is that we're *always* on the 'other side' of the fence!

This story may be useful for:

- Those who need to **re-evaluate** their **priorities.**
- People who are unable to recognise or **acknowledge** their **own skills** and **abilities.**
- Those who **envy** what they perceive others to have.
- People who need to be reminded of their **strengths** and **capabilities.**
- Those who struggle with their own **self-worth.**
- Getting us to rethink our **perception of ourselves.**
- People who **never** seem **satisfied** with what they have.
- Those who are perpetually **unhappy**.

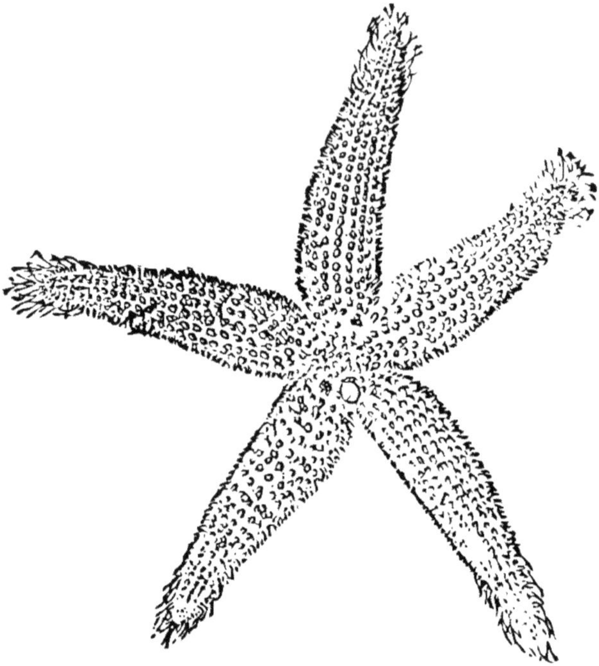

8. Starfish

A young couple were strolling on the beach and enjoying the balmy evening.

As they walked along the shore hand-in-hand they began to notice that there were starfish on the beach. The sand was littered with a tide of beautiful starfish of all shapes and colours that had been washed up by the earlier tide and were now stranded above the high water mark.

"Oh, what a shame!" said the girl. "They're so beautiful and they are all going to dry out and die."

"Well, there's nothing we can do," said the boy dismissively. "There are so many of them. Just watch where you step."

As they rounded the curve in the beach they came upon an unexpected sight. There in front of them was an elderly woman standing at the water's edge and tossing something. As they drew closer they realised that she was bending down and tossing the starfish out into the water one by one.

"Ha! Why are you bothering?" called out the boy. "Don't you realise that's a complete waste of time? There must be tens of thousands of them. You realise of course that you are making no difference at all."

The old woman looked at the small blue starfish in her hand. Slowly and with careful deliberation she turned and tossed it as far as she could out into the waves. Turning to look at the boy she said slowly " Well, it sure made a difference for that one didn't it?"

And then she smiled and bent down to pick up another starfish.

(Source: Unknown)

Possible themes in this story:

Overwhelm - Sometimes we can get overwhelmed by the **big picture** and the task at hand may seem enormous and **hopeless**; so we do nothing.

Focus on what we can do instead of what we can't.

Quitting - It is all too easy to quit. To give up without even making an effort. It takes self-belief and **courage** to continue, especially when faced with a situation that seems vast.

Apathy and **Inertia** - Too often we **choose** to do *nothing* instead of choosing to do *something*.

Excuses - Instead we make excuses. There are those who act and those who make excuses.

Believe in yourself - Just because someone else has an opinion on something that doesn't necessarily make it right for you. If something feels right to you, then do it.

Can *vs* Can't - There will always be those who tell you that you can't. They are generally those who do nothing. We can choose to listen to them or not.

Hope - As long as we keep hope alive we can make a difference.

This story may be useful for:

- ➤ Those prone to **Global (big picture) thinking** are particularly at risk of overwhelm. This is when it is useful to chunk things down to controllable pieces, to do what we can, one thing at a time (ie. to look at only part of the picture to make it more manageable).

- ➤ Those who **fail to take action**.

- ➤ Those who continually make **excuses.**

- ➤ **Procrastinators -** Those who never start.

- ➤ Individuals who let the **opinions of others** influence their decisions and choices.

- ➤ Those who need to **trust** in their **own choices** and actions despite opposition.

- ➤ When people **complain** but take no action themselves.

- ➤ For people who want to **change** but don't know where to begin.

- ➤ **Bullying** - There are many ways of being a **bystander**. All you need to do is to fail to take action by giving yourself the excuse of believing nothing you can do will make a difference. But it's the little things that end up making a lot of difference. One kind word or deed can make all the difference in the world. We may not be able to save the world, but we can make an enormous difference in the lives of those we come into contact with on a personal level.

TELENE CLARKE

9. The Gift

One day Buddha was walking through a village. As he passed through the street a young man began to hurl abuse at him, taunting him and insulting him.

"Who do you think you are?" the young man shouted.

"You have no right going around teaching others like a big know-all. You are as stupid as everyone else. You are nothing but a big fake."

He kept hurling the most awful abuse, each insult worse than the last.

Buddha however, was not at all upset by the abuse. Instead he waited then turned and smiled at the young man and asked him a simple question.

"Tell me, if you buy a gift for someone and that person does not take the gift, to whom does the gift belong?"

"Hah!" said the young man, "What a stupid question. The answer is simple. It would belong to me because I bought the gift!"

Buddha smiled agreeably. "That is correct and it is exactly the same with your anger. If you become angry and direct your anger at me and I do not choose to accept it, then the anger remains yours."

And Buddha continued on his way….

(Source: Zen Parable)

Possible themes in this story:

Reacting to others. We can **choose** to react or not. We can choose to take on the emotions and behaviours of others, or not. We can choose to become insulted, hurt or sad…or not.

Just because someone offers a 'gift' it does not mean that we have to accept it.

Power - When we allow others to '**push our buttons**' we hand them our power. They **control** us. By choosing not to engage there are no buttons to push. It's no fun being **angry** at someone if they are simply not interested.

Bullying in particular requires someone to act the victim. This is a participatory process. By not participating, by not accepting the gift ,the dynamics of this process change.

We can become more **discerning** about the types of gifts we choose to accept. We have a **choice** always about whether we allow someone else's behavior to become part of our experience or not. We can choose to take it on board or we can choose not to.

Other people's **behavior impacts** us. Have you ever been feeling great then someone grumpy comes in? In a short amount of time, if we're not **mindful**, we may feel ourselves becoming grumpy too. This often happens unconsciously We begin to feel different without really being aware of it. What has happened is that you have just been given the gift of grumpiness! Once you are aware that there are gifts that you can't always see you can make a **choice**, you can choose to accept them or not.

Begin to be **selective.** Decide which gifts you want and which ones you don't.

Anger, like all **emotions,** can have a tendency to be contagious. It rubs off onto others. When we are the target of someone else's anger, we may become angry. We may become outraged that they are picking on us; we may become angry back at them or we may feel so riled up or powerless that we go and direct that anger at someone else.

This may be in an overt way (by yelling) or may be less obvious (by being grumpy and snappy at people around us, quite often those who have had nothing to do with the initial episode.)

This story reminds us that we have a **choice**; to take the gift and participate in the process or not.

It is possible to say **no**, simply through not **reacting** or **participating** in any way. Anger is no fun if it doesn't get a response of some kind. To not react takes the wind out of the angry person's sails.

It also reminds us to be **mindful** about what **impact** our own emotions can have on others. Just because we had a hard day at work doesn't mean we need to come home and ruin everyone else's day!

None of us like being around angry people.

By **not engaging** or responding, by not becoming **insulted** or **hurt,** we take the power out of anger. For anger to work it needs a deliverer and a receiver, If you choose not to receive, then it has nowhere to go but back where it came from. We always have a choice about whether to engage or not

Personalising - The abuse and the anger was not about Buddha, it was about the person who delivered it. He may have felt jealous or resentful of Buddha. His value system may have led him to believe that you need to be well-educated to be a great leader. He may have felt **inferior** or **threatened** by Buddha. **Anger, jealousy, resentment**; all are about the *giver* and are a reflection of how they feel about themselves. He was not a happy man and that **unhappiness** was directed outwards. It was not about Buddha. In fact it had nothing to do with Buddha. Buddha recognised that and gave it back to the man.

We can **personalise** things and believe that they are about us or we can recognise that they actually have nothing to do with us and refuse to accept them.

This story may be useful for:

- Those having to live or work with an **angry** person.

- Those being **bullied**. Great for children and teens who need help in deflecting the hurtful words or actions of others.

- **Bullies.**

- People with **anger issues** who are unaware of their **impact on others.**

- As a reminder of the **power of** our own **words** and our emotional state upon others.

- Those who **personalise** things. People who perceive the actions of others to be all about themselves and take it to heart.

- For people who don't **cope** with **conflict.**

- For those with low **resilience** when dealing with the n**egative emotions** of others.

- At times when we need to take personal **responsibility for our actions.**

- To build **discernment skills** in those who find it difficult to distinguish emotionally between what is theirs and what is not.

10. The King And The Boulder

Once upon a time there was a king who called together four of his most trusted men. When they were assembled before him he gave them a very strange order. He requested that under the cover of darkness, they assist him to place a huge boulder in the middle of a roadway. He then hid himself behind some trees and waited until daylight to see if anyone would remove the enormous rock.

Soon the morning traffic began to trail past. Some of the king's wealthiest merchants and courtiers came by and simply walked around the large boulder. Many complained and blamed the king loudly for not keeping the roads clear, but none did anything about getting the stone out of the way.

Then a peasant came along, carrying a load of vegetables to sell at the market. Upon approaching the boulder, the peasant laid down his burden and tried to move the stone to the side of the road. Many people passed by but none offered to assist. Some laughed loudly at his seemingly futile efforts. After much pushing and straining he finally succeeded in rolling the boulder aside. The road was clear once more.

After the peasant had picked up his load of vegetables and was about to resume his journey he noticed a small velvet bag lying on the road where the boulder had been. Curiously he bent down and opened the bag. To his amazement he discovered inside a small fortune in gold coins. Underneath the coins was a note from the king. The note stated that the gold was intended for whomsoever removed the boulder from the road.

The peasant continued happily on his way...

(Source: Unknown)

Possible themes in this story:

We all have boulders and **obstacles** in our lives. We can keep walking around them or we can put the **effort** in to shift them out of the way.

All it requires is for us to make a **choice**; to continue to **do nothing** or to **take action** and do something.

To clear our own path in life and in doing so, make life easier and better for ourselves.

Too many of us are reluctant to deal with the obstacles in our lives.

We are **lazy** and don't want to put in any **effort**.

We want someone else to come along and shift our boulders for us. We want others to **fix** things for us.

Many of us are happy to **stand back** and let others do the hard work.

We are willing to let others step up and **take action** whilst we stand back. Then, quite often we **complain** and get **angry**, envious and **resentful** when we don't get the rewards like they do.

Getting **rewards** often takes effort. That means we need to be willing to experience some **hardship** and some **discomfort**. To get outside of our snuggly little comfort zones and even **risk** becoming a little sweaty and dirty if we want to see a reward at the end of it.

Sometimes, believe it or not, we can actually get to quite like having our obstacles and problems. They become so **familiar** and comfortable that we can become rather attached to them.

We especially like them because they give us great **excuses** about why we can't do things. They stop us from having to take **risks**, to face our **fears** or to take **action.**

It is under the **struggles** in life that we find our real treasures. It is out of **hardship** (like moving boulders/problems/challenges) that we get the **gifts** (learning/lessons/rewards) in life.

We can moan and **complain**. We can blame everyone else for all of our problems and **challenges** or we can step up and actually do something about it. It is a **choice** we are free to make.

We can be a sheep and do what everyone else does (which is quite often nothing) or we can be an **individual** and have the **courage** to step forward and do what we consider to be right for us.

This story may be useful for:

- People who **talk** but never actually do.

- Those who **complain** but are unwilling to take any **action.**

- When someone expects **something for nothing.**

- Those who need to be i**nspired** to take action.

- Reminding us that reward takes some **effort** and action.

- Those who have become so **attached to their story** that they've become unwilling to do anything to change it. (Despite claiming they want to.)

- As a reminder that ultimately **we are responsible** for dealing with the obstacles in our lives.

- Those who are unwilling to be uncomfortable, to step out of their comfort zone.

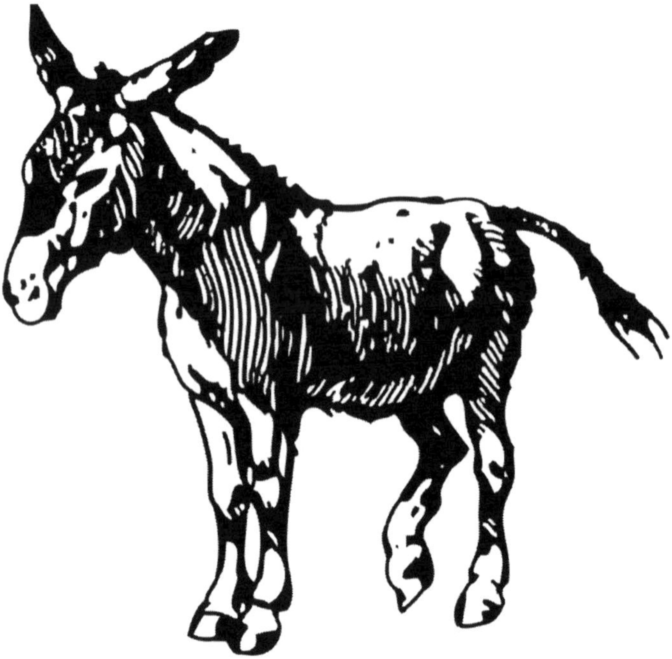

11. Donkey

Once upon a time an old man, a boy and a donkey were going to town.

The boy rode on the donkey and the old man walked alongside.

They were chatting and enjoying the day.

As they went along they passed some people who remarked loudly that it was a shame the old man was walking and the boy was riding.

The man and boy thought maybe the critics were right, so they changed positions.

A little later they passed another group of people who observed "What a shame he makes that little boy walk!"

So the old man and the boy then decided they'd both walk.

Soon they passed yet another group of people who commented rudely that they were stupid to walk when they had a perfectly decent donkey to ride.

So, they both rode the donkey.

Next they passed some people who made them feel ashamed by saying how awful it was to put such a load on a poor donkey.

The boy and man figured they were probably right, so they decided to carry the donkey.

As they crossed the bridge, they lost their grip on the poor donkey.

The donkey fell into the river and was drowned.

(Source: Aesop Fable)

Possible themes in this story:

How often do we allow the voices of **others** into our heads and how often does that directly **influence** our choices?

Sometimes we might be the old man, sometimes the boy and sometimes the donkey. Sometimes it is our **role** to **carry** and sometimes it is our role to **be carried.** The trick is choosing when.

Everyone has an **opinion** and that's okay. Others are as entitled to their opinion as you are to yours. However too often we let the **opinions of others** influence our **decision-making** and our **choices** in a way that is detrimental to our wellbeing or in a way that ends up with us **compromising** what we feel is best for ourselves.

Discernment - We actually have a **choice** about what we take on board from others and what we choose to ignore. We can choose when it is appropriate and useful to take **advice** from others and when to let it go. (This can be quite a revelation to many people.)

Knowing what to **listen** to and what not to listen to. Understanding that just because someone says so, that does not necessarily make it true. Having **discernment** about who to take advice from.

Being an **individual**. Knowing what we want, what we feel is in our best interest and having the **courage** and self-conviction to stick with that.

Having **trust** in yourself. Being able to trust your own **judgment**.

Resisting **feeling pressured** by others.

Trying to **please others**. Being a pleaser, being infected with the 'disease to please' and trying to please everyone, often results in no one being pleased or happy with the outcome. You can **never please everyone**; accept it and then do what you believe is right for you.

Follow your **heart**.

Decision-making - Make your own decisions based on what feels right for you. If something is working for you go with it. Don't simply change something because somebody else has an opinion on it.

What is '**right**' for one may not be right for another.

We are all **different** and that is perfectly okay.

Perspective - There are many different ways to look at things.

Values. We all have different value systems and that affects our view on what is 'right' and what is 'wrong'.

Values are very individual things. We can **respec**t the value systems of others but ultimately we need to decide what fits our own value system and therefore what is right for us.

This story may be useful for:

- **Pleasers -** Those who spend their time attempting to 'keep others happy.'

- Someone who needs to learn how to **think for themselves.**

- Those who **lack trust** in their own judgment.

- Someone who is used to letting **others make decisions** for them.

- Someone who needs to learn how to make their **own decisions** and to be strong in their own convictions.

- Those who allow others to **unduly influence** them.

- **Peer group pressure** situations.

- Those who continually second-guess themselves. People who have **self-doubt.**

12. Losing Everything

Mulla was known as a bit of a joker.

One day he came upon a frowning man walking forlornly along the road to town. "What's wrong?" he asked. The man held up a tattered bag and moaned, "All that I own in this big wide world barely fills this miserable, worthless sack."

"Too bad," said Mulla, and with that, he snatched the bag from the man's hands and ran off down the road with it.

Having lost everything, the man burst into tears and, more wretched than before, continued walking, his entire demeanor now a bundle of misery.

Meanwhile, Mulla quickly ran around the next bend and placed the man's sack in the middle of the road where he would have to come upon it.

When the man saw his bag sitting on the road before him, he laughed with joy, and shouted, "My sack! My sack! I thought I'd lost you!"

Watching through the bushes, Mulla chuckled away. "Well," he said to himself, "That's one way to make someone happy." ☺

(Source: Sufi Story)

Possible themes in this story:

Perspective - Things may appear bad until you discover they can get much worse!

Sometimes a reality check helps us to put some **perspective** on how 'bad' something really is.

Catastrophising - Seeing things as worse than they actually are.

Sometimes it takes a **crisis** to awaken us to what is really important in life. To prompt us to **re-evaluate** and get clarity about what is actually significant to us.

We can wait for the crisis or we can make a **choice** to take a fresh look at the situation and realise that perhaps things are not as bad as we thought they were.

Sometimes it takes us hitting rock bottom, of believing that everything is lost, before we **wake up** and see what we have.

Being a **victim** - By seeing ourselves as a victim, by using victim language we often perpetuate the situation. Essentially, **negative thinking** keeps us in a negative place.

If we want the **situation to change** we need to be able to look at it differently, to gain a new **perspective**.

Often the situation remains exactly the same; we just get to look at it in a whole fresh new way. The situation is **reframed** for us.

Gratitude - Learning to be grateful for what you have.

Having a sense of **humour**. You can choose to cry or you can choose to laugh. The **choice** is yours.

Focus on what you do **have** rather than on what you perceive to be missing.

This story may be useful for:

- ➢ Those who **catastrophise.**

- ➢ Those stuck in **victim thinking** which prevents us from seeing the good side of things.

- ➢ **Negative thinkers.**

- ➢ Those who need to **lighten up** a bit and not take life so seriously.

- ➢ People who **complain** but take no **action** to **change** a situation.

- ➢ Those who are too attached to **old stories** to begin new ones.

TELENE CLARKE

13. Two Wolves

One evening, a Cherokee Elder told his Grandson about a battle that goes on inside of all people.

He said "My son, the battle is between two 'wolves' that live inside us all".

One is evil. It is greed, anger, jealousy and regret. It is sorrow, arrogance, envy, self-pity, guilt and resentment. That wolf is self-righteousness, lies, false pride, bitterness and ego.

The other is good. This wolf is joy, love, hope and peace. It is humility, kindness, empathy, generosity and good intent. The good wolf is compassion, courage, faith and truth.

The Grandson thought about it for a moment then turned to his grandfather and asked curiously "Which wolf wins?"

The old Cherokee simply replied "Whichever one you feed."...

(Source: Cherokee Story)

Possible themes in this story:

Each and every one of us is **human** with the **capacity for good and for bad.**

None of us are **all good** or **all bad.**

No-one is **perfect.**

Acceptance of our own **flaws** and imperfections. Instead of fighting against ourselves, we can accept our **limitations** as being part of ourselves.

We make a **choice,** through our thoughts and our actions, as to which part of ourselves we **nurture** and bring to the world.

Constantly we are put into situations where we make a **choice** with how we **respond**; with our good wolf or our bad one.

Focus - What we focus on grows bigger. If we are focused on our best parts, our **strengths**, then that is what will grow. Focus on the good wolf and it becomes the stronger and more powerful part of ourselves.

If we are focused on our **perceived flaws,** then they will magnify. We begin to **perceive ourselves** in a very **negative** way. When we give our focus and attention to the negative parts they may get worse in reality as well. Things that didn't need to be a **problem** become a problem simply because we are giving them energy and time.

If we can change our **focus** to the **things that are working**, the effective things, the good things, then our experience of reality also becomes better.

The **bad wolf** is the **reactive** wolf, snapping and biting to protect our **ego**, the **shallow** side of us.

The bad wolf has a **need to be right**, to be best at things. It is easily **provoked**, easily upset or hurt. When hurt, the bad wolf tries to get back, to **inflict hurt**.

It spends its time remembering the negatives from the **past** and fearing bad things in the **future**. It is rarely satisfied; wanting with an insatiable hunger, what it sees others having. The bad wolf is always in **pain**. This makes it weak and **unpredictable**.

The bad wolf comes from a place of **fear**, so it covers its fear with **anger**. Underneath what it really wants is to be loved.

The **good wolf** operates from the heart, a place of **good intent**. It has no need to cause hurt. It knows **happiness** and **contentment** come from inside. The good wolf is able to walk in the steps of others, to understand and to have **compassion** for others, yet it has an extraordinary **strength** of its own.

It is able to make strong **choices** that **empower** it, to know when to stand firm and when to simply walk away and **not engage**.

The good wolf is afraid at times, yet has the **courage** to step through the fear. It has no need for violence. It relies on its **intelligence** and on **trusting** its own choices.

Often people refer to **negative emotions** as being **outside of their control**. *("I couldn't control myself.")*

In fact, they are *choosing* to feed the bad wolf. Allowing it to run amok and to stand by and **do nothing**. It is only when we make a deliberate choice to feed and care for the good wolf that we truly become **empowered.**

(Offering up a **challenge for angry people who use the 'out of my control' excuse can be very effective. By bringing into question their **courage** and challenging them to be strong/brave/courageous enough to take on the bad wolf in **battle,** offers a challenge many can't resist. To stop allowing the bad wolf to run their lives and make decisions for them; leaving them powerless in the process, requires them having to be **more powerful** than the evil beast. **Angry young men and boys** often respond particularly well to this challenge and get a great sense of pride in discovering their inner strength and standing up to and conquering the 'bad (ie: weak) wolf.'**)

This story may be useful for:

- **Perfectionists** - People who have the belief that they or others are required to be perfect.

- Those who focus on and are judgmental about their own **perceived flaws.**

- Those who **judge** others.

- People who experience **negative emotions.**

- **Angry** people.

- Those who claim to have **no control** over their own actions and behaviours.

- **Children** who are misbehaving.

- **Children** and **adolescents** who are feeling emotional or conflicted.

- Those who cover their **fear** behind a veil of **anger.**

- Encouraging **focus** on **strengths** instead of perceived 'weaknesses'

- As a **self-empowerment** tool.

14. What Would You Know?

A story is told of the Persian sage Nasrudin, who found himself on the bow of a ferry boat with a pompous intellectual.

As they began conversing Nasrudin said something that the scholar considered ungrammatical.

Bloated with his own learnedness, the scholar began to quiz and criticise Nasrudin's education.

"Have you ever studied astronomy?" asked the pompous Professor.

"I can't say that I have," answered the mystic calmly.

"Then you have wasted much of your life. By knowing the constellations, a skilled captain can navigate a boat around the entire globe."

A few minutes later the learned one asked, "Have you ever studied meteorology?"

"No I haven't."

"Well then, you have wasted most of your life," the academic scolded. "Methodically capturing the wind can propel a sailing ship at astounding speeds."

After a while the condescending fellow inquired, "Have you ever studied oceanography?"

"Not at all."

"Ah! What a waste of your time! Awareness of the currents helped many ancient peoples find food and shelter."

A few minutes later Nasrudin began to make his way toward the stern of the ship. On his way he nonchalantly asked the fellow, "Have you ever studied swimming?"

"Haven't had the time," the professor haughtily responded.

"Then I'm afraid you have wasted all of your life – the boat is sinking."

(Source: Sufi Parable)

Possible themes in this story:

Life education *vs* School education. Often we **value** one over the other or **judge** others on standards that are purely subjective and not necessarily valid.

Context - Just because something works and is useful in one situation it doesn't necessarily follow that it will work or be useful at all in another.

Feeling **superior** to another may not always end well.

Judgment - We judge others based on our own value systems. In doing so, we often overlook what they have to offer or what we can learn from them.

Everyone's knowledge is valuable.

We all have different skills, knowledge and abilities. There will always be a time and a place where these unique things are invaluable. There will also be times and places where they will be of no use whatsoever.

Being an **expert** is very context dependent.

Becoming **over-confident** can be risky.

This story may be useful for:

- ➢ Those who believe they are not 'educated' enough, who **feel inferior** because of a perceived **lack of formal education.**

- ➢ Those who believe that they are not skilled enough, smart enough or talented enough or who constantly **compare** themselves with others.

- ➢ Those prone to **arrogance.**

- ➢ Those who are **judgmental** of others.

- ➢ **Perfectionists**. Those seeking to be 'experts.' Who believe they never quite know enough.

- ➢ **Procrastinators**. Those who use the excuse of not being skilled enough to actually start something.

15. Duck And Chicken

A married couple were walking along one evening, both relishing the opportunity to take some time out to enjoy each other's company and to take in the beauty of the setting sun.

As they strolled hand in hand, talking tenderly to one another, there was a sound off in the distance.

Quack! Quack!

"Oh, listen!" said the wife. "Did you hear the chicken?"

"Ha! Darling, that was actually a duck," said the husband affectionately, laughing at her mistake.

"No it was a chicken," stated the wife, looking at him in surprise. "I know what a chicken sounds like!"

"It was most definitely a duck," said the husband, a look of disbelief beginning to show on his face "Chickens make a *Cluck! Cluck!* sound and that was most certainly a *Quack! Quack!* I think there must be something wrong with your ears tonight my love!"

"Well it sounded exactly like a chicken to me!" the wife insisted. "I *know* It was a chicken and there is nothing wrong with *my* ears."

"Well I am 100% positive it was a duck," said the husband, beginning to grow more and more irritated.

Quack! Quack!

"See? I told you! It's a duck! Listen…"

"No dear, I'm sure it's a chicken. We used to have chickens when I was little. It was a chicken," said the wife digging in her heels.

"Listen here! It is a DUCK!!" shouted the man angrily. "D-U-C-K…DUCK! Got it? It is a DUCK! Stop being so ridiculous!"

The wife was almost in tears by now. "But I'm sure it's a chicken…" she said, more meekly this time, but still determined to be heard.

Quack! Quack!

The man was red-faced and livid by now. "Can't you hear that?! It's a duck you…you…."

Finally, the man looked and noticed the tears in his wife's eyes and all of a sudden he remembered why he had married her. His face softened immediately and composing himself, he said gently "My darling, I am so sorry. You heard right. I think it is a chicken. Forgive me for upsetting you."

She smiled up at him and reached over and took his hand, holding it tenderly. "Thank you honey."

The happy couple once more looked at each other with love in their eyes as they continued their evening stroll.

As they walked, they heard;

Quack! Quack!.

(Source: Ajahn Brahm)

*(**Alternative Version:** Gender can be changed as to who is 'wrong' and who is 'right.')*

Possible themes in this story:

The most important thing in life is **love**.

Having our **buttons pushed**. Allowing ourselves to be **annoyed** by others.

Needing to be right. Ego is a wonderful thing. Our need to be right is a basic human driver. We can engage with it constantly or we can save it for the important things.

Who actually cares if it is a chicken or a duck? Sometimes we get so caught up in our **need to be right** that we forget what really is important. The walk together, the harmony, the love they felt towards each other, the enjoyment of being together, of enjoying their evening walk; were all far more important. Too often we get caught up in pointless and damaging arguments and begin acting more like adversaries than people in love.

Prioritising - Knowing what is **important** and worthy of our time and attention and what is not.

Perspective - Discerning the mountains from the molehills. Don't sweat the small stuff.

Point of view - Sometimes it's all about how we look at things. In my mind it is one thing, in your mind it is another. Who is to say who is right?

Consider the possibility that the woman grew up in a family where all of the poultry was referred to as *chickens*; sort of a generic term. Therefore, in her mind she is 100% right. All *quacks/berks/clucks and cock-a-doodle-doos* are made by '*chickens.*' That is what she learned as a child so that is what she has continued to believe.

What is **truth** for you may be different for me…and that's okay.

Apologising - Having the ability and the self-esteem to be able to apologise, even when you know you're 'right'.

When we are not coming from ego with a need to be right, we are able to apologise without **resentment**, even when it is 'not our fault.' We simply don't have so much of ourselves invested in the outcome.

Accepting that an **opinion** is simply an opinion. Not **personalising**.

Reacting with emotion versus **responding** with mindfulness.

Conflict is normal and doesn't have to be conflict.

There are going to be times when we **disagree** with others.

There are going to be times when others disagree with us.

There are going to be times where we are sure we are **right** and someone else is **wrong**.

In close relationships we can go from being totally 'in love' with someone in one moment and then fighting over the smallest of things in the next instant and detesting the person we adored five minutes before.

Instead of feeding conflict and making it bigger and worse, we can recognise that it is human and **normal** to **disagree** and it is also a **temporary** state… if we so choose it to be.

Often when we **disagree** it may begin a **pattern** that starts with **catastrophising**. We take an insignificant disagreement then blow it out until it has moved from '*chicken or duck*' to '*Are we actually meant to be together?*' A common way we do this is by using a **snowball effect**. We start with one little thing then keep adding, bringing in other annoyances, past disagreements, old incidents (either in our minds or out loud) until it's escalated from a trivial point of difference to a major conflict. We also **generalise** so it permeates and taints everything. ('He *always* disagrees with *everything* I say' / 'She *never* listens when I try to tell her something.')

Too often we get caught up in the **details**, those small things that annoy us, and we lose sight of the big things, the **important things.**

Compromise is an important facet of every relationship.

However, although there are times when it is okay to back down, there are also times when it is necessary to **stand up for yourself.**

This requires **discernment**. Knowing when to go into battle and when to surrender.

It is not simply about giving in, it's about knowing WHEN to back down and when to stand tall and be **assertive**. Of having the skills to be able to identify what is and what is not **important**.

There needs to be **balance**, not simply one person conceding and one 'winning'.

Some things are better left unsaid. It's a matter of being smart enough and discerning enough to recognise which things they are.

Being mindful of the **impact** of your words on others.

Sometimes we get it wrong even when we're certain we are 100% right!

This story may be useful for:

- **Couples** bickering or being caught up in a battle of the egos.

- As a **re-focus** tool to get attention away from the small things and back onto the more important issues. (Eg: why people got together in the first place.)

- Those who always **need to be right**.

- Those who need to become more **assertive**.

- Those who **avoid conflict**.

- Those who find it difficult to **apologise**.

- **Angry** people.

16. The Fisherman

An executive from the big city was holidaying in a Mediterranean fishing village. As he walked alongside the harbour, he noticed a fisherman unloading his catch, checking his nets and whistling cheerily. He got chatting to the fisherman and began quizzing him on his life.

"This seems like such a quiet place," he said. "What do you do all day?" "Well," said the fisherman, "I sleep late, go out and catch a few fish, spend time with my family and in the afternoons I rest. In the evenings we often meet in the town square to catch up, share a few drinks, make music and indulge in good conversation. I am a happy man."

The executive's keen eye however had noticed the quality of the catch and he asked the fisherman how long it had taken him to gather such a fine bounty.

"Not long at all," replied the fisherman.

"These are fine fish," said the executive, his business mind ticking over as he looked at the fisherman's simple boat. "But there are so few here. Why didn't you stay out and catch some more?"

"Why would I do that?" asked the fisherman. "There's more than enough here to sell and to feed me and my family."

"Well, it would be a good thing to simply stay out a little longer and catch more fish. With the added proceeds you would be able to buy a much better and bigger boat."

The fisherman looked at him quizzically.

The businessman continued. "With the proceeds from the bigger boat you would soon have enough to buy several boats. Eventually you would have a whole fleet of fishing boats. Then, instead of selling your catch to a middleman, you could sell directly to the processor; eventually opening your own processing factory. That would give you control over the product, the processing and the distribution. In that way you could grow your business, eventually moving it offshore and expanding into other countries. You could set up headquarters in New York or L.A. where you could oversee your expanding business enterprise. You could make an absolute fortune!"

"Hmmm," said the fisherman, "And how long do you think this will all take?"

"Oh," replied the businessman, "Fifteen to twenty years at the most."

"Then what?" asked the fisherman.

"Well, that's the best part", said the executive excitedly. "When the time is right, you could launch it on the Stock Exchange and sell off stock to the public and become even wealthier. You could make millions!"

"And then what?" asked the fisherman.

"Well, then you could retire, move to a seaside village somewhere, sleep late, fish a little, spend time with your family, catch up with friends, share a few drinks, enjoy some good conversation."

The fisherman simply smiled and went on mending his nets.

(Source: Unknown)

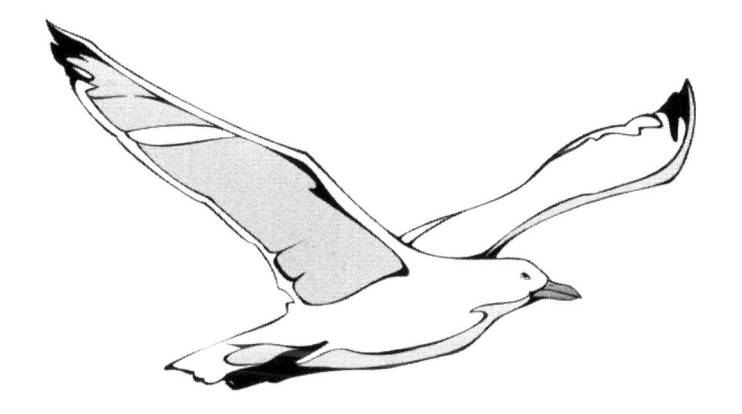

Possible themes in this story:

Live NOW! Don't stake everything on some far off time that may never eventuate. Sure we need to plan ahead, but it's what we *do in the meantime* that really counts.

Sometimes we **make life complicated** when it doesn't need to be.

Keep life **simple**.

Often we go **searching** for things that we **already have**.

Things and money don't necessarily bring **happiness**.

Sometimes we **give advice** where it isn't needed or asked for.

Enjoy what you **have**.

Values - Knowing and being clear about what is *really* **important** to you. So often value systems are imposed on us and we do what we feel we *should* do, what we feel is **expected** of us, rather than what we'd really like to do.

Purpose - What is important to me? Money? Family? Partner? Children? Community? Spare time? Business success? Too few of us stop and ask ourselves this most important question, yet it is the one that guides us on our journey through life.

We can float aimlessly in life or we can have a

destination to head toward.

Life balance - Sacrificing relationships, time with our children and partners, to accumulate wealth or to 'be successful'; all at some magical time in the future. Remembering to make time to enjoy life and create balance.

Having the **courage** to follow what is true for you, despite the pressures to **conform.**

Choose **happiness now.**

This story may be useful for:

- **Workaholics.** Particularly those who sacrifice their relationships with those closest to them with the excuse that they are accumulating wealth 'for the family.'

- Those who need to **stop and reflect** on values/ beliefs/ attitudes.

- Helping gain **clarity** around **life purpose.**

- To promote discussion around **priorities** and what is **important** in life.

- Someone whose life is out of **balance** in regard to work/ family/ fun.

- Those who are in need of a life change or **career change.**

- Those who may **feel stuck.**

- People who appear to be **never satisfied** with what they have

- Those who **postpone happiness**

- Individuals who **live in the future** instead of being in the **present.**

- People in a relationship with someone whose

values do not match and where this creates disharmony or conflict. Where each has **different priorities.**

➢ **Busy** people.

➢ **Stressed** people.

➢ An individual whose **value** system and **priorities** are **impacting negatively** on those around them.

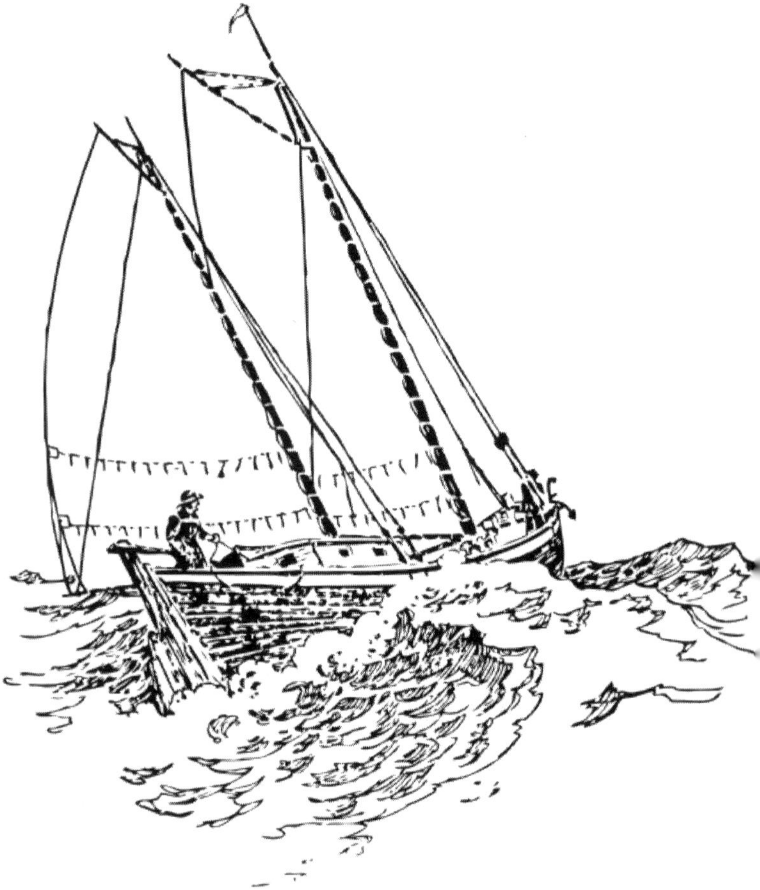

17. Good Luck, Bad Luck

Once there was a farmer who had worked hard on his farm for many years. He did not own very much but he did have a strong horse.

One day the horse ran away.

Upon hearing the news his neighbours came to visit. They shook their heads sympathetically. "What bad luck," they said.

"Maybe," replied the farmer.

The next morning the horse returned, bringing with it three wild horses.

"How wonderful!" exclaimed the neighbours. "What good luck!"

"Maybe," replied the farmer.

The following day the farmer's son tried to ride one of the wild horses. He was thrown from the horse's back and broke his leg.

The neighbours arrived to show their sympathy for the farmer's misfortune.

"Such a terrible incident," they commiserated. "What bad luck!"

"Maybe," replied the farmer.

The subsequent day the military arrived in the village. All of the young men in the country were to be drafted and sent away to war. As the farmer's son was incapacitated with a broken leg he was spared and remained behind.

"What good luck!," said the neighbours congratulating the farmer on his family's good fortune.

"Maybe," replied the farmer.

(Source: Zen Parable)

GOOD LUCK, BAD LUCK

Possible themes in this story:

Perspective - Sometimes things may seem awful or disastrous. At times situations or events may seem so disastrous we may believe it is an 'end-of-the-world' scenario. However, with hindsight, things turn out to be not so bad after all.

Instead of **reacting** instantly, of making immediate **judgments** and **assumptions,** it is often a better idea to simply hold neutral space and see what unfolds. Very often things turn out to be so much better than we **expect**.

As humans we have a tendency to find a **negative perspective** on things and predict **negative outcomes** that often do not eventuate.

Worry is a futile exercise; 98% of the things we worry about do not eventuate in the negative way we forecast. (*And incidentally, 97% of statistics are made up on the spot!*)

Patience - Wait to see what happens instead of acting as if it already has.

Being in the **now**. Being **mindfully present** in whatever life brings.

Acceptance – Things are what they are. Simple acceptance of this can make our lives far **less stressful**. We can fight and **resist** the inevitable or we can simply accept that sometimes that is how things are and simply get on with life.

Attempting to **control** what happens. Acceptance involves acknowledgement that sometimes things are simply outside of **our control**.

Catastrophising - Making mountains out of molehills.

Perspective/Point of view - We all have different ways of seeing things….and that is perfectly okay!

Silver linings - Sometimes 'bad' situations can actually be a blessing in disguise.

This story may be useful for:

- Those who **react** without thinking.

- Those who act, speak or make **decisions** without having all of the **relevant information.**

- **Worriers** - Those who experience **anxiety**. (ie. who are always projecting negative outcomes into the future.)

- Those prone to **negative thinking.**

- To encourage **mindfulness** and a focus on the present.

- As a reminder that we can all make **different meaning** from the same events or situations.

- Reminding us that **attitude** is everything.

- People who seek to **control** everything in their life.

18. The Six Blind Men And The Elephant

The six blind men met weekly to catch up and enjoy good conversation.

One warm day, they began discussing this wondrous thing they'd often been told about, called an elephant. Each had heard about what an unusual beast the elephant was yet none of them had ever had a direct experience of the strange creature. Although each personally believed they had some idea, they agreed to find an elephant and discover first hand what the animal was really like. Setting off to a nearby market the six blind men were soon directed to an elephant.

The first blind man tentatively approached the beast and put out his hands to feel the elephant's firm flat side.

"It seems to me the elephant is just like a wall," he declared to his friends.

The second blind man stepped forward and his hands found one of the elephant's tusks. "No," he said firmly. "The elephant is round and smooth and sharp. The elephant is just like a spear."

Intrigued, the third blind man reached out and he encountered the elephant's trunk. "Well, I can't agree with either of you. The elephant is a squirming and writhing thing. The elephant is, in fact, very much like a snake."

The fourth blind man was of course by now quite puzzled. He reached out and wrapped his arms around the elephant's leg. "All three of you must be completely mad," he said, "Because the elephant most obviously is very much like the trunk of a tree."

Utterly confused, the fifth blind man stepped forth and grabbed hold of one of the elephant's flapping ears. "How can you all be so mistaken?" he demanded. The elephant is nothing like that. It is of course, exactly like a fan."

The sixth blind man came forward. Holding onto the elephant's tail he disagreed loudly with them all. "You are all crazy! It is nothing like any of your descriptions. The elephant is in fact, just like a rope."

And, as they set off down the road, the blind men continued to argue about just what an elephant was like; each of them completely wrong and yet, each of them completely right.

(Source: Old Indian Tale)

THE SIX BLIND MEN AND THE ELEPHANT

Possible themes in this story:

Each of us has a completely different **worldview** that relates directly to our own **unique** experience of 'reality'.

There is never just one way of **seeing** something, no matter how obvious or black and white it may seem to us.

What is truth? Our truth and another's truth may be very different experiences.

Truth depends on who is looking. Our experience of the world is filtered through such things as our **beliefs**, our **values**, our past experiences and our **attitudes**. Everyone's version of truth is unique.

Perspective - We can all have the same view in front of us but each of us can 'see' something different.

Right *vs* wrong - You can be right and wrong all at the same time.

We are often blind to the fact that another's **opinion** can be **different** to our own and yet still be right.

Some of us spend our entire lives being blind to this fact.

Often we only see **part** of the whole. Too often we grab hold of a tiny piece of something and believe that we have the **whole picture**. We don't realise that we only have hold of the ear or the tail, yet we're convinced that we intimately know the whole elephant.

**(This is a great metaphor to develop a common language around. Instead of arguing and trying to be 'right', we can agree that I'm seeing an ear and you're seeing a leg. Both are parts of the same elephant, but we're having a different experience of it.)

'Details' people (ie. **specific thinkers**) often get bogged down in the specifics of situations. They become so fixated on examining the trunk that they forget that it's attached to an enormous elephant.

We need to know and accept all of the parts to know and **accept** the **whole**.

Conflict - Too often we come involved in conflict that is totally pointless and illogical, simply because we are driven to hold onto and defend our own **points of view.** We involve ourselves in arguments in the constant drive to feed our **ego** by proving that we are 'right'.

Often this results in ill-feeling and **fractured relationships** and friendships.

Being willing to **open** your **mind** to accept other **possibilities** and **perspectives.**

There are **many roads** to the **same destination**. I might take the route of the leg and you may take the trunk but in the end we both end up knowing the whole elephant.

Life is about gathering all of the **pieces** needed to create the whole picture.

This story may be useful for:

- People in **conflict situations.**

- Those who have a **need to be right.**

- Individuals who find it difficult to accept the **opinions or views of others.**

- Those who may need others to see things their way and cannot understand or tolerate why they can't.

- **Specific thinkers** (or nitpickers) who get obsessed with detail and lose sight of the big picture.

- In **mediation** situations – eg. to locate **common threads** to unite and pull people together. To remind people that they are actually working toward the same big picture and have the same goals.

- **Teamwork** situations. An elephant is made of parts. All parts are of **equal importance** and all go toward making up the whole elephant.

19. What Will It Be Like?

One day a traveller was walking along the road on his journey from one village to the next. Wandering along he noticed a monk working in a field alongside the path. As he got near the monk looked up and smiled, greeting him with a cheery good morning. The traveller nodded in reply then stopped in front of the monk and said "Do you mind if I ask you a question?"

"Of course not," replied the monk, "Ask away!"

"Well, I am travelling from the village in the mountains to the village in the valley and I was wondering what it was like in the village in the valley?"

"Hmmm, tell me," said the monk, "What was your experience of the village in the mountains?"

"Oh it was just awful," replied the traveller. "To be perfectly honest I couldn't wait to get away from there. I found the people to be most rude and unwelcoming. From the moment I arrived the people were cold and unfriendly. I was never made to feel part of village life no matter how hard I tried and the people made it very clear that they do not take kindly to strangers. In fact, I found it a most unpleasant experience. So tell me, what can I expect in the village in the valley?"

"I see," said the monk. "I am sorry to tell you, but I think you will find that your experience in the village in the valley will be much the same as the one you had in the last village."

The traveller sighed loudly, hung his head despondently and walked on.

A day or two later, another traveller was journeying down the same road and he too came upon the monk.

"Excuse me please," he called out. "I am travelling to the village in the valley. Do you know what it is like there?"

"I do", answered the monk, "But first, tell me where have you come from."

"I have come from the village in the mountains," replied the second traveller.

"And how did you find it?" asked the monk.

"Oh it was a fabulous experience," cried the traveller. "I would have stayed there forever if I could! I have never been made to feel so welcome anywhere. The village people treated me as though I was a member of their family. Everyone was so kind and generous. The elders took time to share their wisdom, the children laughed and joked with me and I was made to feel part of all community activities and events. It was so sad to have to leave but I will always carry special memories in my heart and hope one day to return. And, what of the village in the valley?" he asked again.

"I think you will find it very much the same," replied the monk. "Good day to you."

"Good day to you and thank you very much," the traveller smiled before journeying on.

(Source: Zen Parable)

Possible themes in this story:

Our experience of life is what we make it. We do that through the **attitude** we bring to our everyday experience of life.

Essentially we create our own reality. What we **expect** is what we get. Whatever we 'put out there' we will be verified on the outside. We unconsciously validate our own **beliefs** and **expectations**.

People who believe that most teenagers are lazy, will look about and spot only lazy teenagers. Those who believe that all plumbers are overpriced, will always find plumbers who overcharge them and those who believe that the majority of people are unfriendly, will always encounter unfriendly people. We **attract** that which verifies our deep-seated (and often unconscious to us) beliefs.

Attitude is everything. Two people can have an identical experience and see it in completely different ways. It all depends on what we **focus** on and what we are **open** to.

Having **expectations** results in us being open to **disappointment**. If we have no expectations, no preconceived ideas, then we are more open and receptive to what is.

Having **unrealistic expectations** leads to constant disappointment.

Living in the future, being **anxious** or **worried** about the future, often takes that **negative emotion** into our future experience.

Often we base our **expectations** of future experiences on **past experience**. We **generalise** one experience and map it across to others, including those that have not yet happened. One bad experience becomes the blueprint for future experiences. Your one encounter with a nasty bearded man makes you forever wary of bearded men. In some contexts this can be useful, in others it prevents us from being **open** to **new** and better **experiences.**

Our **happiness** is not the responsibility of others. Others do not exist to make us happy. Our happiness lies solely in our own ability to find happiness within ourselves. This is then reflected in those around us.

This story may be useful for:

- **Negative thinkers.**

- Those who experience **anxiety** or **worry** unnecessarily.

- Those with high or unrealistic **expectations of others.**

- Those who believe it is the **role of others** to make them happy.

- Those who **blame others** for what is not right in their world.

- Those who like to **control** their world instead of experiencing it.

- People who have had a **negative experience** or **trauma** and as a consequence, have developed a belief around that which prevents them from being open to new experiences.

20. The Black Door

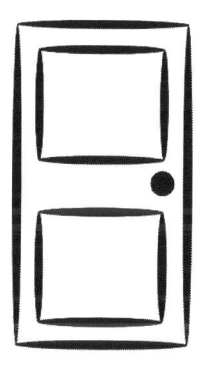

The young man was a prisoner of war. Like others before him, when the time came, he was brought before the Persian General in order to determine his fate.

The young man was certain of death, but as he stood there, the Persian General generously gave him two choices. On the young man's left was the firing squad, guns poised ready at their sides. On his right was a plain white wall, in the middle of which was a large black door.

The choice was simple. The young man was given leave to determine his fate; the firing squad or the black door.

The young man duly made his choice and shortly after, a volley of shots rang out and the prisoner crumpled to the ground.

The General shook his head and began to walk away, commenting as he did so to his aide, that in all of his years, he had seen very few men choose the black door.

"May I ask Sir?" the aide queried, "What lies beyond the black door?" "Freedom," the General replied. "The black door leads to freedom yet very few choose it."

"Why is that?" asked the aide looking puzzled.

"Because most of us are terrified of the unknown," replied the General. "Most would rather choose a fate we know, even if that means death rather than face the uncertainty of the unknown. Those who have the courage to walk through the black door deserve to be free."

Source: (Source: Unknown)

Possible themes in this story:

Human beings **crave the familiar**. Quite often we would rather hold onto what we have rather than **experience something new**; even if what we have is **limiting** us or **depriving us of happiness**.

We stay in **unhappy marriages**, we work in jobs we hate and we experience 'life' as a series of groundhog days; same follows same follows same....

We are unwilling to let go of the familiar to take the **risk of the unknown-** even if it promises us something better.

Being **afraid of change**.

Being **afraid of 'different'**.

Courage - Making **choices**, taking **risks**, facing the **unknown** all requires courage.

Facing the unknown, even if that means embracing uncertainty and the discomfort of 'not knowing.'

Taking risks - To grow, to live fully requires that we take risks; even when we are very **afraid** and don't know what the **outcome** will be.

Being **prepared to fail.** Every choice contains a risk of **failure**. So does making no choice.

Comfort zones - Holding onto the what's easiest and familiar, even if it is second rate.

Letting go of the past - It is only when we are willing to let the past go completely that we can be totally free to move forward into something new and better.

Trust in ourselves - Taking a risk requires that we have trust in ourselves and in our own abilities. Without that trust, we find it difficult or even impossible to let go of what we have in order to **experience something new.**

This story may be useful for:

- ➢ Those who are looking for **something more from life.**

- ➢ People who are **afraid to take risks.**

- ➢ Those who won't leave their **comfort zone.**

- ➢ When needing to make a **choice.**

- ➢ Those who **fear change.**

- ➢ In **decision-making** situations.

- ➢ When needing some **courage** to step forward in life.

- ➢ For someone who **feels stuck** or trapped in a negative situation Eg: domestic violence, unhappy marriage or job.

QUICK GUIDE INDEX

(Topic – Story Number)

Acceptance 4,7,8,11,12,13,15,17,18,20

Anger 1,9,13,15,18

Anxiety 3,5,6,12,13,17,19

Assumptions 2,5,8,10,11,12,14,15,17,18,19

Attitude 1,2,3,5,6,7,8,9,10,11,12,13,14,16,17,18,19

Beliefs 2,5,8,10,11,12,14,15,17,18,19

Blame 3,5,7,9,10,11,12,13,15,18,19

Boundaries 9,11,15

Bullying 1,4,8,9,11,13,14

Challenges 1,4,6,8,9,10,12,13,15,17,20

Change 1,2,8,11,12,13,20

Choice 1,3,5,8,10,11,17,20

Conflict 9,13,15,18

Control 3,9,13,15,17,18,19

Courage 1,5,7,8,9,,10,11,13,16,20

Decision- Making 1,3,5,8,10,11,17,20

Failure 3,10,12,15,20

Fear 1,5,9,10,13,20

Habits 1,2,8,11,12,13,20

Happiness 3,6,7,12,13,16,19,20

Helpers / Rescuers 4,11,16

Hurt 9,13,18

Judgment 7,8,11,12,13,14,15,16,17,18,19

Life Balance 3,16

Making Excuses 3,5,7,9,10,11,12,13,15,18,19

Mindfulness 2,5,9,15,17

Negative Thinking 3,6,10,12,13,19

Opinions of Others 6,8,9,10,11,16,17

Optimism 5,6,8

Peer Group Pressure 8,9,10,11,14

Perfectionism 13,14

Personal Strength 1,5,7,8,9,,10,11,13,16,20

Perspective 1,2,6,7,8,9,11,12,15,16,17,18

Positive Thinking 5,6,8

Procrastination 3,8,10,14,16

Resilience 1,4,9,10,11,12,13,17

Risk 3,10,12,15,20

Self- Confidence 1,3,4,5,6,7,8,9,11,13,14,20

Stress 3,4,12,16

Taking Action 1,2,3,4,5,8,9,10,12,13,20

Taking Responsibility
3,4,5,8,9,10,11,12,13,15,17,19,20

Trust 4,7,8,11,12,13,15,17,18,20

Unhappiness 3,6,7,12,13,16,19,20

Values 3,6,7,8,9,10,11,12,13,14,16,18

Worry 3,5,6,12,13,17,19

ABOUT THE AUTHOR

Telene Clarke had her first books published in 1994.
She has over 30 years experience working as an educator, counselor and coach with children, adolescents and adults.
Telene writes for a number of on-line health programs and is currently working on a range of new books for both adults and children.
She lives by the seaside in South Australia.

Printed in Great Britain
by Amazon